French Country Cottage *Seasons*

Courtney Allison

Gibbs Smith

For my parents, my husband,
and our children and grandchildren.

Introduction

From the chill of winter with frost-covered leaves to the camellia tree wrapped in delicate pink flowers, each season offers its own beauty and wonder, inviting endless opportunities to decorate the home with the inspirations of nature.

Spring transforms dainty buds into beautiful, abundant blooms while the first flowers of the year are opening up in the garden. In summer, the greenhouse garden becomes fruitful with foliage, as blackberry vines and climbing roses mingle with the more orderly flower beds. Autumn changes the landscape with the draping of golden hues and fallen leaves as chunky pumpkins adorn the scenery. Winter brings a softer view, with most of the plants resting for the season. But even on those chilly days, the hellebores, daffodils, and tulips start to grow and bring a burst of sunshine to the frosty landscape.

While the scenery outdoors changes dramatically as the year goes on, my favorite way to add a touch of seasonal bounty inside the house might surprise you. It doesn't involve big transformations, like changing furniture or redecorating every part of a room. I have learned that bringing in the more natural, subtle changes speaks the most to me. It's the accents, the delicate touches that add character through simplicity, like the gathered goods you find while roaming the garden. It's the mundane pieces, such as freshly clipped flowering branches, lush greens, pine cones, moss, or maybe even fruit from the tree. All simple in nature, but when woven together, they whisper a beautiful story full of seasonal charm in their own way.

This book is filled with glimpses of moments in our home and garden like that, showing you how you can weave together your own seasonal beauty in big and small ways. Through these pages, I hope that you find inspiration to seek the magic that nature offers and to create a home and lifestyle that nurtures you each season.

An autumn bouquet created with wheat, dried flowers, and fresh roses tied with a ribbon is a lovely centerpiece for a table or mantel display.

Spring

Awakening & Renewal

When the sunrise is accompanied by the sound of wild birds greeting me with their melodies, I know spring is in the air; I love to stay in bed just a little longer to savor the magic of their singing.

After the chilly days of winter, the warmth in the garden renews my spirit as spring flowers begin to rise from the ground and the trees bud out. Buds become blossoms on fruit trees, new leaves decorate branches, and blooms begin to dot the flower beds that were covered in frost only weeks ago. As we move closer to summer, longer days with both spring rains and warm sunshine bring new growth in the garden, transforming it with layers of lovely.

In California, we have many flowers that blur the lines between seasons, with their blooms lasting from one season into another. Our camellia tree starts to bloom in winter and keeps adding beautiful flowers into spring. In the garden, wisteria and lilac are some of the earliest spring bloomers, along with the 'Cecile Brunner' roses that ramble over the arches and fences. The peonies, climbers, garden roses, foxgloves, larkspur, and many others are not far behind. Together, they create a flower story in the potting shed garden as the season moves toward summer.

Inside our home, spring sunlight splashes through the French doors and dances across the floor, bringing new inspirations and warmth to our space. Fireplace mantels are adorned with fresh blooms, and a flower-filled wreath greets guests at the door, while the kitchen island often has a large arrangement of whatever is blooming in the garden.

Aside from the plentiful blooms that inspire me this time of year, spring often gives me a literal spring in my step; it has always been a special time for gathering with loved ones and making new memories. Think indoor tables with floral-filled cloths and arrangements, fresh fruits, and homemade seasonal desserts that bring a feeling of brightness to the table. This could also be tables set outdoors where seasonal flowering trees, bushes, and gardens create lush backdrops, while the scent of garden blooms floats through the air. Truly, spring is a captivating season to get more creative with colors, branch out with fresh stylings, and weave together your daydreams with a sprinkle of nostalgia to captivate all who come to your tables.

When the camellia tree is in bloom, it becomes a beautiful spot for a spring moment with an antique chair tucked under the branches.

Spring Home

PAGES 14–15: A table for two set by the spirea in bloom is a lovely spot for a spring soiree.

OPPOSITE: A bouquet of garden roses, peonies, and lisianthus creates a whimsical moment on a chair.

PAGE 18: Inside a cupboard, a small arrangement of tulips adds a seasonal touch.

PAGE 19: Coral peonies placed into a green bucket bring a burst of late spring cheer the kitchen.

COOPER • The Prairie

An arrangement of larkspur, spirea, and foxgloves from the garden holds a commanding position on the dining table.

PAGE 22: A vintage wooden bucket is an ideal vessel for making a statement with tall flowers.

PAGE 23: A birthday cake and bouquets await placement on the table, while baskets aplenty find comfortable storage in the kitchen.

ABOVE AND OPPOSITE: Dainty arrangements of garden roses set in small vintage vessels are gathered on the mantel with stacks of books and candles for a touch of spring cozy.

PAGES 26–27: I love a mingle of tall and low floral arrangements. In the bedroom, the mantel decor has both. Tall purple larkspur and vibrant magenta statice deliver a burst of color, while soft pink roses add undeniable elegance.

Spring Entertaining

A cheesecake for a special celebration gets a little extra sweetness with roses, peonies, and a birthday banner. *(See page 41 for Protocol for Decorating Food with Fresh Flowers.)*

PAGES 30–31: Spring ushers in outdoor gatherings. This table celebrates the season with layers of flowers on the vintage cloth and in the arrangement for a picture-perfect setting under the oak tree.

HAPPY
BIRTHDAY

Our old growth camellia tree creates a magical backdrop for a spring gathering. This tree begins blooming in winter and the flowers continue to open well into early spring. One of the things I love about camellia trees is the long-lasting carpet of pretty petals they leave underneath after the spent blooms have dropped—another layer of lovely.

PAGES 34 AND 35: A blue gingham cloth and a bouquet of camellia blooms create a lovely spring or Easter setting. The vintage Franciscan Desert Rose place settings were my great-grandmother's and bring a special nostalgia to the table.

ABOVE AND OPPOSITE: A table indoors is lovely set with candles, dainty plates and cloths, and fresh garden roses.

OPPOSITE: On the table, a bouquet of delightful cream peonies and blush roses echoes the 'Cecile Brunner' rose beauty and brings a quiet, romantic touch to the rustic table.

ABOVE: At the front courtyard patio is an arch where 'Cecile Brunner' roses create a stunning display each spring. We planted these about twenty years ago, and they grow more magnificent each year.

Artisan Breakfast Sandwich

2 slices fresh-baked artisan bread

1 egg

1 slice meat (optional)

Slice of cheese (we love melted brie, but use what you prefer)

1 avocado, pitted and sliced

A handful of fresh lettuce

1 heirloom tomato

1/4 onion, sliced

Salt & pepper, to taste

Crushed red pepper, to taste

Drizzle of blue cheese or ranch dressing (or your preference)

Fresh basil leaf, whole or chopped

Toast the bread, if you wish. Cook the egg as a scramble or however you'd like. If you are including a meat, you can cook it at the same time. Once the egg is ready, turn off the heat, but leave egg in pan and place cheese on top; cover to let melt for a minute or so.

Smash the avocado onto the toast and add egg on top. Layer the lettuce, tomato, and onion. Sprinkle with salt and pepper and red pepper to taste. Drizzle with the dressing, add basil garnish on top. Add remaining slice of bread and cut sandwich in half. Serve warm.

Fresh Flower-Garnished Pie

Fresh garden roses with blueberries and blackberries create a nostalgic look for this bakery apple pie. Choose any variety of pie you like.

Garden Roses

Blueberries

Blackberries

Barrier for placing on pie

Protocol for Decorating Food with Fresh Flowers

Whether making your favorite apple pie or cheesecake from your grandmother's recipe or stopping by the bakery for a fresh-made dessert, something that always adds sweet charm to the table is using flowers to decorate the top.

While fresh flowers are always lovely, if you decide to use fresh flowers as garnish on any type of food, there are some very important things to know:

1. Only use food-safe flowers. This is critical to remember, and you always need to do diligent research to be sure you choose 100 percent food-safe flowers before adding them—even if you are just setting them on the top for garnish. A tip is to ask your local bakery, as they have knowledge on safety and often sell food-safe fresh flowers or can source them for you.
2. You always want to use only organic flowers. Wash and dry them well. Even in a food-safe flower, non-organic and unwashed flowers may have pesticides on them.
3. Another favorite way to enjoy fresh flower garnishes is to wrap the stems in florist tape, especially covering the stem ends and any cuts from which liquid might seep. Place a small barrier on your dessert before setting your flowers on top to prevent the flowers from directly touching the food. Simply remove the flowers and barrier when serving.
4. Alternatively, wonderful sugar flowers and realistic faux flowers can give you the look.

Bits of magical moments spotted in spring.

ABOVE LEFT: A blush vanity by the camellia tree was perfect for whimsical photo shoots.

ABOVE RIGHT: Sweet little Louis, a naked neck frizzle rooster, loves to come indoors and keep me company while I am working.

BELOW LEFT: Long velvet ribbons tie the flatware together on the table.

OPPOSITE: An antique carriage house door is backdrop for a plop of pretty blooms on a chair and a jar holding a broken stem from the garden.

Spring Florals

This spirea grows abundantly in the spring, its branches arching over and through the picket fence. Cascades of dainty white flowers make a perfect spot for inspired-moment photographs.

PAGES 46–47: Fresh-clipped garden roses tucked into a vintage basket are a delightful centerpiece for a spring table by the rose-covered garden arch. Elegance in simplicity.

A mingled arrangement of various grocery store blooms and foraged bits is a whimsical look for spring.

BELOW LEFT AND PAGES 52–53: How to turn a purple cabbage into a beautiful floral centerpiece in just a few steps:

- Carefully carve out the center of a cabbage to create a "vase" large enough for florist foam to be tucked inside. Add water and let it soak.
- Clip your flower stems, leaving some longer to overflow a bit.
- Tuck the stems into the florist foam to hold their place and arrange until you are happy with the bouquet. Fill in bare areas with dainty blooms like dianthus and stock.
- Add in bits of greenery underneath as needed.

OPPOSITE: The simple table for a small Easter gathering is set in the sunroom, where vintage lace curtains filter an abundance of warmth and light. Pastel colored Easter eggs are stacked in a vintage tureen, and the place settings are a mingle of vintage elements.

Spring Garden

The spring garden receives plenty of rain and sunshine, so by mid-spring, layers of blooms fill the beds and pathways, while peonies and roses are ready for clipping.

PAGES 56–57: A blooming picket fence moment. Larkspur mingling with foxgloves creates a magical view behind the picket fence. In the background, lilac and 'Cecile Brunner' roses add more blooms, and in front of the fence, the garden roses are putting on new growth.

A different perspective of the 'Cecile Brunner' roses growing along the back of the ivy wall. They have grown tall enough to reach the pergola on the other side and now drape down between the boards, creating magic in spring.

PAGE 60: Foxgloves are among my favorite flowers in the cottage garden and in pots and planters as well.

PAGE 61: A well-worn bench by the spirea is a lovely spot to sit and soak up the sunset.

OPPOSITE: A group of terra-cotta planters bloom with grape hyacinth and herbs. Planting grape hyacinth in pots is a lovely way to enjoy their pretty purple blooms in early spring

ABOVE: In the potting shed, bulbs and herbs planted in winter are nearing bloom. The terra-cotta swan planter was a yard sale find; though it is a bit crumbly in places, it charmed me and I had to bring it home.

PAGES 64–65: In the greenhouse garden, beds are filled with a deluge of blooming flowers in spring. This view is looking toward the path where the foxgloves, peonies, and roses have a stronghold.

S

ummer

Long Days & Golden Evenings

Summer brings early morning coffee in the garden among the flowers, golden sunshine splashing through our French doors, and warm evenings with dinners set under starry skies.

Our garden is full of lush new growth reminiscent of a fairy tale. Ruffly garden roses take center stage as the foxgloves and peonies start to fade in early summer. Our wild sweet peas bloom and cover the back of our property with pretty little purple flowers, while our climbing roses are covered in blooms, and the garden grows in wild profusion. The roses grow tall, reaching the top of the cherub fountain by midsummer, continuing to bloom into autumn.

In our home, adding summer bounty here and there, rather than a ton of detailed decor, is what speaks to me. Sometimes it is a single type of flower, like peppery scented roses in a jar on the mantel, a pitcher by the sink in the bathroom filled with that morning's garden bounty, or a bucket of tall blooms on a side table that welcomes you to pause a moment. Other times, it's fuller displays that mix some of the newest blooms from the garden with fresh greens to create an array of untamed yet delicate beauty. And when the flowers start to fade and drop petals, I tie them with twine to hang from beams in the kitchen and enjoy their beauty in another season.

While summer brings splendor to our home and garden, it also brings plenty of opportunities to host gatherings outdoors. With nature putting on a show and creating lush backdrops, setting a table on the path through the sweet peas or at the top of the garden by the potting shed sets the stage for an awe-inspiring gathering that is sure to fill the hearts of all who join. It's hard not to be captivated by the layers of fresh blooms this season brings, the serene summer colors that weave through our home, or the sunny days that invite you to wander the garden and savor the beauty that summer offers.

Clippings of barely blushing roses from the garden are held by a simple jar on the kitchen windowsill.

PAGES 70–71: Juliet roses interplay with pretty purples for a happy soak in the sink.

Summer Home

A garden bucket filled with stock and larkspur is simply gorgeous on a side table.

PAGES 74–75: Tall bundles of larkspur alongside shorter jars holding dahlias accentuate the vintage blue-and-white plates on the dining table.

RIGHT: Dried flowers hang on open beams above the antique kitchen sink in the cottage, adding a country-style charm.

PAGE 78: A mix of fresh and dried flowers overlook foraged acorns and glowing candles.

PAGE 79: Flowers have inherent beauty at every stage of their existence—just like we do.

PAGE 80: A dressy upholstered vintage chair is right at home with my collection.

PAGE 81: In the laundry room, thrift store find barkcloth floral curtains cover the work areas, while a dainty gilded chest creates a little spot for flowers in this small space.

OPPOSITE AND ABOVE: At the top of the little attic stairs, a jar filled with hollyhocks and roses echoes the vintage floral pattern on the bedding for a sweet touch.

PAGE 84: I have a weakness for dainty gilded pieces like this small chest of drawers. I tuck them wherever they'll fit, and they almost always hold a petite floral arrangement.

PAGE 85: A medley of seasonal blooms in the bathroom adds a touch of summer between the sinks.

Summer bedding is lighter and brighter in shades of whites, creams, and dainty florals. The pop of color on the vintage sofa brings a burst of sunshine.

Summer Garden

An antique chair holds a dainty vintage silver pitcher of fresh-cut garden roses.

The summer garden sometimes gets a little wild and woolly. I find it charming, in an overgrown storybook cottage kind of way, and aside from tucking stray bits aside to be able to open the door, we let the rambling vines do their thing.

OPPOSITE: A basketful of freshly cut wild sweet peas and garden roses wait to be arranged.

ABOVE: The garden beds grow in layers each season.

RIGHT: Gathering sweet peas by the fence.

PAGE 94: Snaps of magic-filled moments.

The cherub fountain amid garden roses; garden blooms on repeat; chickens wandering the garden with us.

PAGE 95: Layers of late spring into early summer blooms caress the picket fence.

PAGES 96–97: Our garden paths bloom profusely in early summer. The interplay of foxgloves, garden roses, and the last of the peonies is truly magical.

Summer Entertaining

OPPOSITE: Vintage floral plates echo the flowers in the centerpiece and bring a nostalgic charm to a summer table.

PAGES 100–101: Our sweet peas grew in such abundance, I was mesmerized by their beauty. I set a long narrow farmhouse table on the path to create a gathering tucked in among their magic.

PAGES 102–103: Just a few roses with hollyhocks were perfect for a simple summer floral arrangement.

PAGES 104–105: A pair of vintage cherub statues became a centerpiece for a summer table with the addition of vases and bottles of flowers.

PAGES 106–107: I collect vintage pieces like flatware, glassware and floral plates all year long and mingle mismatched pieces for a unique look. This table set on the garden path by the potting shed was filled with magic and an abundance of floral scent.

Spaghetti Squash Bake

1/4–1/2 spaghetti squash per person
3–4 cloves garlic, minced, or more to taste
1 medium onion, chopped
6–8 ounces mushrooms, sliced
2 teaspoons olive oil
Cooked vegetarian crumbles or cooked ground meat (optional)
1 tub ricotta cheese
1 cup fresh spinach
1 jar traditional pasta sauce
3 ounces Parmesan cheese, grated
1/2 cup grated mozzarella cheese, or to taste
Italian seasoning, to taste
Salt and pepper, to taste
Fresh bread, warmed, and butter, for serving

Preheat oven to 400°F.

Cut each spaghetti squash in half and scoop out seeds. Place upside down on a baking sheet with a little water added, and bake for about 30 minutes, or until you can insert a fork into it.

Meanwhile, sauté garlic, onion, mushrooms, and seasonings in olive oil. Add faux crumbles or meat, if desired, and cook with the vegetables. Add ricotta and spinach; then mix everything in with the spaghetti sauce and cook until heated through.

Remove squash from oven when fully cooked. Fill spaghetti squash boats with a generous amount of the sauce mixture. Top with Parmesan, mozzarella, and seasonings.

Return to the oven and bake until cheese melts. Serve with warmed bread and butter.

Fruit-Topped Cake

Whether you start from scratch with your favorite cake recipe, order ready-to-decorate rounds from your local bakery or simply garnish a ready-to-serve cake for a quick customization, adding fresh berries is a delicious way to enjoy the flavors of summer and create a beautiful sweet treat for the table.

3 (12-inch) white cake rounds

3 cups white buttercream or whipped icing

Fresh berries of your choosing—blackberries, blueberries, strawberries,* raspberries; plan on 1 to 2 containers of each berry for a three-layer cake

Garnishes: fresh sprigs rosemary, oregano, or thyme

*I used Driscoll's trademarked Rosé variety of strawberries for this cake.

Bake your cake or pick up pre-made rounds from the bakery. I use three 12-inch layers for a tall cake, but you may prefer more or less.

Wash and dry the berries and herb sprigs and set aside. If using fresh flowers, be sure they are organic, food-safe flowers. Wash and dry each flower and set aside.

Place the first layer of cake on a platter and spread a generous layer of icing on top. Add the next cake layer and icing.

Cover the top layer of cake with a thick layer of icing, and then start arranging the fruit. I start with the largest pieces, which are the strawberries, then fill in with blackberries, blueberries, and raspberries. Ring the cake with berries on the platter.

Arrange optional garnishes.

Summer Florals

OPPOSITE: A happy bucket of summer blooms is perfect anywhere you place it.

PAGE 112: I adore these ruffled peonies when they are fully open.

PAGE 113: Roses in shades from dark to light are supported by lisianthus and statice, all tightly grouped in a brass punch bowl.

PAGE 114: A happy combination of farmers market flowers in a silver pitcher is a profusion of color: lisianthus, dahlias, asters, roses, and others.

PAGE 115: A pitcher with a mingle of sweet peas and 'Eden' climbing roses on a vintage wood chair creates a moment in the sweet peas.

Autumn

Cozy Nights & Gatherings

Autumn winds usher in moody colors, crisp air, and foggy mornings. I relish snuggling up close to the fire as layers of yellow and orange blanket the evening horizon.

In early autumn, the golden grasses and first colorful pumpkins begin to emerge in the garden. Our apple trees are full of rose-colored fruit, blackberries are plentiful, and acorns and hazelnuts begin to dot the ground beneath the trees. Our front door welcomes guests with cornstalks and a wreath or a bunch of flowers tied with a ribbon. Morning walks in the crisp air bring delight as the tree foliage turns from green to bold crimson and vibrant oranges. As the season moves closer to winter, the steps of the house, barn, and potting shed are overtaken with pumpkins and seasonal foliage.

While I love the bold colors outdoors, inside I lean toward the softer side of autumn and the muted colors that nature provides. Natural touches like wheat and grasses, dried flowers, heirloom pumpkins, gourds, and foraged bits like acorns and dried foliage are woven all through my home. Pumpkins are stacked by the fireplace, while dried flowers from summer are turned into garlands for the mantels, with pine cones or acorns sprinkled here and there.

A Thanksgiving table set indoors by the fireplace can be stunning. But outdoors in nature, the table is enchanting with bouquets accented with foraged ferns and dried sweet peas, gathered moss and lichen, fallen chestnuts, or a cornucopia filled with seasonal bounty. Pumpkin bouquets filled with flowers such as hydrangeas, dahlias, and roses from the garden become centerpieces, and string lights overhead keep the table lit long into the evening.

Overall, autumn is a season of joyous celebration, of interplay between vibrant tones and muted ones, and taking time to pause and notice the changes around us. Whether it's the carpet of leaves crunching underfoot, the toasty feeling of flames in the outdoor fireplace, or the comforting sensation of wrapping your hands around a warm mug, it's an optimal time to breathe in calmness and immerse yourself in the moment.

Sweet Curly, our house rooster, enjoys the cozy fire. The mantel is arrayed in dried foliage and flowers, orange slices, and velvet ribbons, which will last all season long.

Autumn Home

OPPOSITE: A harmony of the seasons unfolds in an autumn pumpkin floral arrangement with an underpinning of winter garland.

PAGE 122: A blend of dried grasses and flowers draws the eye wherever they are placed—as an accent in a floor arrangement, on a mantel, or as a table centerpiece.

PAGE 123: Mellow warmth from candles, dried foliage, and chubby heirloom pumpkins are staples of autumn in our home.

PAGE 124: A seasonal moment in the kitchen is warm with a dried wreath, a stack of heirloom pumpkins, and a few bits of autumn foliage.

PAGE 125: A bucket of sunflowers on a checked linen cloth in the entry signals the shift from summer to autumn.

PAGES 126–27: The bedroom is all about restful colors and warm layers. A vintage flower-filled duvet and ruffled pillows dress the bed, while a dried foliage garland on the mantel and a golden candle beside a silver pitcher of seasonal blooms on the nightstand create a quintessential autumn ambiance.

PAGE 128: In the attic, vintage floral bedding and stacks of extra pillows create cozy warmth on the beds.

PAGE 129: Simple gathered branches dotted with fruit and drying leaves decorate a living room mantel.

PAGE 130: A welcoming front porch means lots of muted heirloom pumpkins and clusters of mums. Curly followed me while we were working; I am always taking breaks to cuddle my chickens.

PAGE 131: Bundles of cornstalks around the door make a splendid frame for a botanical bunch of dried flowers tied with a velvet ribbon.

PAGES 132–33: I am often inspired by patina and enjoy using pieces in unexpected ways. An old carpenter's chest with well-worn paint and filled with metal trays is a unique vessel for flower arrangements.

Autumn Entertaining

OPPOSITE: A pop of bold orange flowers in a vintage metal container is a striking seasonal centerpiece. Single blooms with dried flowers in glass vessels echo the loveliness.

PAGES 136–37: Autumn brings color in foliage and blooms. These dahlias from farmers bunches were divided into dainty containers. The commons of purple, peach, and pink in small vintage crystal decanters created a blooming centerpiece.

PAGES 138–39: A large heirloom pumpkin inspired this gorgeous fresh floral arrangement of seasonal blooms. We hung a large chandelier for light and a bit of drama over the table for a gathering under an oak tree.

PAGE 140: A chocolate cake wears dainty chamomile flowers.

PAGES 144–45: Before the hazel tree drops its leaves and nuts, its arching branches make a canopy over a little hollow, a spot to escape to. The addition of vintage mushroom stools and a table conjured a fairy-tale moment amid the freshly fallen oak leaves, while a bouquet of garden roses and a few candles made the mood romantic.

PAGES 146–47: The potting shed is distinctive in every season, but especially in autumn with pumpkins and mums covering the steps. We set up an autumn table in front and layered it with a tartan throw as a cloth, apples and acorns that had fallen, and a bouquet of dried seasonal flowers studded with crimson foliage.

Caramel-Drizzled Apples with Almonds

1 (10-ounce) bag salted caramels
2 tablespoons water
4 Granny Smith apples
1 cup chopped almonds
4 skewers and 4 sticks (optional)
Large cupcake baking cups

Unwrap caramels and place them into a saucepan with 2 tablespoons water.

Heat the caramels over low-to-medium heat and stir continuously until they are melted.

Skewer an apple and dip it in the caramel, turning the apple to coat it fully. Wait for a minute and dip a second time if desired; then place on a cupcake baking cup. The caramel will drip off the apple as it sits, so the baking cups will help to catch it. Repeat with remaining apples.

Drizzle more caramel on the top of the apples in a zig zag form. Then sprinkle with chopped almonds and lightly press them into the caramel. Replace skewers with a small rustic stick if you wish.

Cool in refrigerator for 10 minutes to set. Serve at room temperature.

Hearty Split Pea and Butternut Soup

1 (16-ounce) package green split peas
2 tablespoons olive oil
1 medium onion, diced
3–5 cloves garlic, chopped or minced
1 pound baby red potatoes
1 cup chopped carrots
1 cup chopped celery
1 cup diced butternut squash
1 tomato, diced
4–6 small pie pumpkins, or sugar pumpkins (one per person)
1 cup fresh super greens or favorite greens
Salt and pepper to taste
Grated Parmesan cheese, for garnish
Crusty baker's loaf, sliced and warmed

Bring 6–8 cups water to a boil; add in the peas and olive oil and bring to a boil again; then reduce heat and let simmer.

After 20 minutes, add the onion, garlic, potatoes, carrots, celery, squash, and tomato to the pea soup mixture and simmer until peas are tender, about 45 to 60 minutes.

Meanwhile, slice the tops off the small pumpkins and scoop out the seeds. Bake the pumpkins at 350°F for about 1 hour, depending on sizes, or until just barely tender; then set aside.

When the peas and veggies in the soup are fully cooked and tender, add the super greens to cook for a few minutes. Add salt and pepper to taste.

Ladle soup into the baked pumpkins and top with grated cheese.

Serve with crusty warm bread.

Black lace cloth sets the tone for a moody table full of Halloween magic and concoctions. Vintage pieces like candelabras, black goblets, and a brass punch bowl emphasize the mood. The centerpiece is created with dried botanical bits and sugar-covered fruit. Ghostly figures and specters can be imagined in the drippy wax candles on the table and in floating candelabra attached to the pergola with fishing line. We hung them slightly askew for extra spookiness.

Autumn Florals

OPPOSITE: An antique settee moment with a dried flower arrangement.

PAGE 152: Hops, dried sunflowers, ferns, and mixed dried floral bunches make a charming arrangement in a vintage urn.

PAGE 153, CLOCKWISE FROM TOP LEFT: An arrangement of dried flowers and fresh-clipped blackberry foliage is a blend of early autumn bounty; bushels of potted mums are always on repeat at French Country Cottage; dried hydrangeas overflow a vintage swan planter; a variety of colorful dahlias making a stunning cluster.

PAGE 154: A pumpkin filled with dried flowers, fresh flowers, and vining foliage comes together in a slightly unruly yet appealing way.

PAGE 155: A gathering of wheat and dried flowers is accented with fresh roses and tied with ribbon.

Autumn Garden

The barn is ready for a gathering with stacks of heirloom pumpkins on the steps and candles on the table inside. The chandelier all aglow forecasts an uncommon kind of party for the guests.

OPPOSITE: The greenhouse garden is decked out for the season.

THIS PAGE: Our chickens follow us pretty much everywhere we go.

PAGES 160–61: The Avion trailer has been turned into a pumpkin patch just right for autumn festivities.

PAGES 162–63: Setting out a basket of apples from our tree, stacking pumpkins, and tucking in candles on the steps is the easiest way to decorate. Easy, natural touches of the season are my favorites.

FARM FRESH
PUMPKINS

ABOVE: A weathered vintage basket cradles bright golden sunflowers.

OPPOSITE: Inside the potting shed, bunches of dried flowers are tied to fallen tree branches used as rods.

ABOVE: On a table by the French doors, the cornucopia platter waits to be moved to the table and creates a lovely moment framed by the red foliage of the plum tree.

OPPOSITE: A lush Thanksgiving centerpiece, the cornucopia with a bounty of fruit is paired with a bouquet of flowers and turkey transfer-ware plates on a checked cloth.

PAGES 172–73: Vintage plates and a brass champagne bucket of flowers mingle with a scattering of pears, plums, figs, and a few chestnut pods gathered from the ground.

Les Faisans

Les Cailles

A moss centerpiece on the table creates a lovely ground for a pair of figurine birds, candles, and a pitcher of seasonal blooms.

Winter

Nurturing & Celebrating

Winter ushers in a softer kind of beauty, one that draws a cozier feeling into the home. Outside, the landscape grows quiet. Bare trees stand against overcast skies, and chilly nights lay a gentle frost across the grass and evergreens.

Though many garden blooms are resting, the landscape is far from barren. Blackberry branches tangle with colorful rose hips, and early potted bulbs and herbs begin to fill the beds. Even when rain, hail, or snow makes an appearance, hardy daffodils and hellebores offer bright bursts of cheer. By late winter, camellia buds unfurl, covering the tree in layers of pink blossoms and bringing a touch of storybook beauty.

Indoors, winter is a season of nurturing all who live and gather here. Our pace naturally slows to a gentle simmer, and I savor mornings spent sipping coffee by the glow of a crackling fire. In the evenings, candles cast their warmth, and chairs layered with throws invite lingering. The heady fragrance of potted paperwhites or the soft scent of peonies in pitchers drifts through the rooms. As nature rests, I gravitate toward a softer palette indoors—pale blush, creamy whites, and dusty lavender—accented with gathered mossy branches, pine cones, and evergreen clippings.

Winter also opens the door to celebration. Twinkling trees, tinsel, and rhinestones scatter a bit of magic throughout the house. The dining table moves closer to the living room fireplace, where fresh greens and flowers form a lush centerpiece and candles add a warm glow. Outdoors, a farm table in the greenhouse creates an intimate scene. When weather allows, a table and chairs are gathered beneath the oak, adorned with whimsical touches such as a crystal chandelier suspended from its branches.

Whether through spirited holiday decor that stirs nostalgia or the quieter side of the season expressed in subtle hues and cozy layers, winter invites us to add an extra measure of love to our homes—traditional and unexpected touches along the table, shimmers of light among the baubles, and foraged bouquets that create gatherings guests will not soon forget.

For a special winter party, the staircase is styled with fresh flower garland on the railing and candles on the stairs.

Winter Home

OPPOSITE: The dining table is moved close to the warmth of the fireplace for a festive winter gathering.

PAGES 182–83: Peonies are a treat in winter and are luxurious on the table or the mantel with a few pine cones and candles.

PAGE 184: A cozy chair and vintage floral ticking–covered sofa across the living room from the fireplace create a spot to enjoy the ambiance of the season.

PAGE 185: This mantel styling started with a plain holiday garland and was customized with flowers and foliage. Poppies, grasses, hydrangeas, and other florals were tucked into the garland and became a luxurious decor look for the season. Realistic faux taper candles are safer to use near dried foliage, while an abundance of fresh magnolia leaves and garden roses are tucked in for freshness and a warmth.

THESE PAGES: A pair of peony arrangements on the long dining room table are a simple and welcoming look for the holidays and all winter long.

PAGE 188: In the bedroom, the mantel is decorated with a Christmas garland full of foliage and baby's breath that I left in place to dry after the holidays. A dainty pitcher of pink flowers and vintage brass candlesticks tied with ribbon create a romantic look.

PAGE 189: Cozy candles and the vintage chandeliers dimmed low create a lovely light for arranging winter blooms.

PAGE 190: A vintage ladder holds candles and flowers for soothing ambiance in the bathroom.

PAGE 191: The guest bedroom is layered with vintage floral patterns in linens and pillows. An antique wall mirror is covered in patina, its mottled glass reflecting the linens in the French armoire across the room.

Winter Entertaining

OPPOSITE: Holiday tables don't always have to be indoors. The oak tree has been fitted with a plug and a long cord for the chandelier; it can be tucked out of sight when not in use.

PAGES 194–95: This outdoor holiday table has pizzazz! On the antique table, I paired the fresh-and-faux garland with vintage blue-and-white plates, crystal glasses, and assorted flatware. Vintage lace napkins and flatware tied with ribbons complete the settings.

ABOVE: The same table in a simplified version is also fit for a fête. *Tip:* Favorite place settings can be paired with different centerpieces and decorative elements to create a range of looks.

OPPOSITE: In a lusher look for a holiday table, the fresh cedar garland has jars of peony arrangements, blush mercury glass ornaments, and a vintage lace cloth. Blue-and-white plates are a favorite any time of year, as are vintage floral plates in mixed patterns.

Butternut & Beet Salad

- 1/2 butternut squash, cut in half
- 1–2 large fresh beets
- 1/2 medium red onion
- 4 cloves fresh garlic (if desired)
- 2 tablespoons extra virgin olive oil
- 2 cups fresh spinach
- 1/2 cup crumbled feta cheese (if desired)
- 1/2 cup pecans, chopped of halved
- Salt & pepper to taste
- Balsamic vinegar drizzle (if desired)

Clean, peel, and chop the butternut squash, beets, red onion, and garlic. Place chopped vegetables in separate bowls to prevent beets from staining the others.

Heat oil over medium-high heat. Sauté squash first separately to prevent it from getting stained. When squash is partially cooked, add chopped garlic to the pan and finish cooking together. Transfer back to the bowl that held the squash. Sauté beets next. Sprinkle all vegetables with salt and freshly ground black pepper to taste.

Wash the spinach and layer on your serving platter.

Top spinach with chopped onion. Spoon squash with garlic onto spinach. Add beets then sprinkle with cheese and pecans. Chill if desired. Drizzle with balsamic vinegar before serving.

New York Style Cheesecake

1 cup graham cracker crumbs

3 tablespoons sugar

3 tablespoons margarine, melted

Filling:

3 (8-ounce) packages cream cheese, softened

3/4 cup sugar

3 large eggs

1 teaspoon vanilla

Optional garnishes: 1 1/2 to 2 cups fresh blueberries or organic, food-safe fresh or faux flowers

Preheat your oven to 325°F.

Combine graham cracker crumbs, sugar, and melted margarine in a bowl and mix until well blended, no dry crumbs. Press mixture onto the bottom of a 9-inch springform pan and bake for 10 minutes.

Remove crust from oven and raise oven temperature to 450°F.

To make your cheesecake filling:

Combine cream cheese and sugar in a large bowl and mix with an electric mixer at medium speed until well blended. Add eggs one at a time, mixing well after each addition. Blend in the vanilla and then pour filling into crust.

Bake at 450°F for 10 minutes; reduce heat to 350°F and bake for 25 to 30 minutes more, or until set.

Loosen cake from rim of pan by running knife around the edges. Cool cheesecake for at least an hour before removing the rim. Chill in the refrigerator at least 4 hours while it firms.

For optional garnishes, add several handfuls of fresh blueberries, if desired, once the cheesecake is cool, or top with food-safe fresh or faux flowers for a festive touch. *(See page 41 for fresh-flower safety.)*

Winter Florals

OPPOSITE: Hellebores are a lovely winter flower. We have about a dozen of them planted around the greenhouse, where they bring a burst of happy to the winter garden and when brought indoors for arrangements.

PAGES 202–203: White flowers of any variety seem to shine brightly in winter indoors. Peonies or garden roses with eucalyptus provide layered luxury, while potted and force-bloomed narcissus contributes an intoxicating scent to its space. Grouped pots have powerful impact. Don't forget to embellish the "ground" beneath them.

PAGES 204–205: An inspired moment: an antique trunk for a photo shoot became a lovely little spot to plop a few armfuls of peonies. The pairing of rustic with elegance is a hallmark of French country style that appeals to my soul.

Winter Garden

Tulips planted in pots can be forced to bloom early, just like paperwhites. In the garden, they bring a burst of color to the other early-blooming plants in the beds.

The winter potting shed is all about planting bulbs outdoors for spring flowers and in pots for forcing winter blooms to take inside.

Winter Festivities

OPPOSITE: A magical moment with sweet little Curly, our house rooster, in front of a tree dressed in nothing but twinkling lights.

PAGE 212: A welcoming front door wreath decked in layers of ribbon and pine cones welcomes guests into the coziness.

PAGE 213: This dainty tree was placed inside an antique brass punch bowl and decorated simply with vintage ornaments. Moss was tucked around the top of the pot. Ribbons and rhinestone garlands draped from the table and the sconces provide extra layers of sparkle and magic.

Christmas

OPPOSITE: A sparkling tree full of layers of ribbons and vintage ornaments glows in the corner of the living room. The vintage statue wears pearl and rhinestone garlands as a necklace. Her crown was made with fresh juniper and cedar foliage and small vintage ornaments.

ABOVE: Inside an antique cupboard, candles and fresh-clipped cedar with orange slices bring a cozy Christmas touch that will last all through the holiday season and into the new year.

THESE PAGES: Bright pink baubles provide a lively contrast to this vintage tinsel tree. Our exclusive-design ruffled floral tree skirt is layered with packages wrapped in old newspaper. The sweet vintage sheep adds a bit of whimsy; originally designed as a footstool, it now serves as a lovable touch anywhere it is placed.

PAGE 218: A whimsical presents table holds packages waiting to be gifted. This tree is nestled inside a fresh pine wreath with cedar branches and moss tucked in for a lush woodland look. Velvet ribbons on the sconces and dainty ribbons on the tree balance the rustic look with a bit of softness.

PAGE 219: A festive country-style New Year's Eve brunch table with a bouquet of blooms and a flower-topped dessert welcomes the year ahead.

New Start

In the greenhouse, a festive table is set for celebrating New Year's Eve. Stools are gathered around an antique farm table enhanced with fresh garland. An assortment of place settings with ribbons and candles aglow weave down the table, exuding a magical ambiance for welcoming in a fresh new year.

Acknowledgments

My deepest gratitude goes to the following:

My family, for inspiring me to create and do what I love every day. I love each of you very much.

Raymond, for supporting my crazy ideas, tending the gardens, keeping me fed when I work late, and helping with the setup and cleanup of all the whimsical stylings.

Ansley—my mini-me and assistant—for helping me create, making me laugh, and managing so much behind the scenes while I'm capturing the magic.

Ryan and Cullan, for your help with editing, advice, and unwavering support, along with your loves, Katt and Diem. And to our littlest loves—Juliette, Enzo, Jionni, Sophie, Jio, and Sienna—who bring so much joy to our family and inspire me to create seasonal magic for them.

My parents, for nurturing my creativity from the time I was a little girl, and for your constant love and support. Seasons and celebrations were filled with the magic you created while we were growing up, and those memories inspire me to create the same for my family.

My siblings, for always supporting my creative ventures.

Jill Cohen, Madge Baird, Rita Sowins, and my Gibbs Smith family, for your friendship, encouragement, and support as we worked together to create another beautiful book.

My brand partners, who have become like family, and my readers, who have become dear friends.

Our *French Country Cottage* community, for reading my blog, sending notes, supporting my books and creative projects, and stopping by to say hello and share a hug at signings. *French Country Cottage* would not be what it is without you.

The Author

Courtney Allison founded the lifestyle brand and blog *French Country Cottage*, a place inspired by renovations of her 1940s cottage and about living a lifestyle that is fueled by inspiration and the romance that comes with it. She loves the quintessential mix of rustic and elegant elements, indulges a love of all things sprinkled with ambiance and magic, and believes that a chandelier and bouquets of fresh flowers belong in every room.

In addition to working as an influencer, she is a freelance photographer, stylist, and floral designer. Her work has been featured in magazines and websites in the U.S. and Europe.

A mom of three grown children and a grandmother of six, Courtney lives in a little slice of the countryside in California with her husband and their flock of silkie chickens and a pair of mischievous goats. She loves to travel and discover new inspirations, taking camera in hand, playing with flowers, and creating moments of whimsy. Connect with Courtney and French Country Cottage on her blog, Facebook, and Instagram.

Other books by Courtney Allison:
French Country Cottage
French Country Cottage Inspired Gatherings
French Country Cottage Christmas
French Country Cottage in Bloom

First Edition
30 29 28 27 26 5 4 3 2 1

Published by
Gibbs Smith
Layton, Utah
www.gibbs-smith.com

The authorized representative in the EEA is Simon and Schuster Netherlands BV, Herculesplein 96 3584 AA Utrecht, Netherlands, info@simonandschuster.nl

Designed by Rita Sowins / Sowins Design

Library of Congress Control Number: 2026930010
ISBN: 978-1-4236-6261-7

Printed and bound in China using FSC® -certified and other controlled materials.

FSC
www.fsc.org
MIX
Paper | Supporting responsible forestry
FSC® C208677